Living to please God

1 THESSALONIANS

by Mark Wallace

Living to please God
The Good Book Guide to 1 Thessalonians
© Mark Wallace, 2005. Reprinted 2010, 2013, 2016, 2018, 2019, 2021.
Series Consultants: Tim Chester, Tim Thornborough,
                              Anne Woodcock, Carl Laferton

Published by:
The Good Book Company

thegoodbook.com | thegoodbook.co.uk
thegoodbook.com.au | thegoodbook.co.nz | thegoodbook.co.in

ISBN: 9781904889533 | Printed in India

CONTENTS

Introduction: Good Book Guides

Every Bible-study group is different—yours may take place in a church building, in a home or in a cafe, on a train, over a leisurely mid-morning coffee or squashed into a 30-minute lunch break. Your group may include new Christians, mature Christians, non-Christians, mums and tots, students, businessmen or teens. That's why we've designed these *Good Book Guides* to be flexible for use in many different situations.

Our aim in each session is to uncover the meaning of a passage, and see how it fits into the "big picture" of the Bible. But that can never be the end. We also need to appropriately apply what we have discovered to our lives. Let's take a look at what is included:

⊕ **Talkabout:** Most groups need to "break the ice" at the beginning of a session, and here's the question that will do that. It's designed to get people talking around a subject that will be covered in the course of the Bible study.

⊕ **Investigate:** The Bible text for each session is broken up into manageable chunks, with questions that aim to help you understand what the passage is about. **The Leader's Guide** contains **guidance on questions**, and sometimes ⊗ additional "follow-up" questions.

⊕ **Explore more (optional):** These questions will help you connect what you have learned to other parts of the Bible, so you can begin to fit it all together like a jig-saw; or occasionally look at a part of the passage that's not dealt with in detail in the main study.

⊕ **Apply:** As you go through a Bible study, you'll keep coming across **apply** sections. These are questions to get the group discussing what the Bible teaching means in practice for you and your church. ⊕ **Getting personal** is an opportunity for you to think, plan and pray about the changes that you personally may need to make as a result of what you have learned.

⊕ **Pray:** We want to encourage prayer that is rooted in God's word—in line with his concerns, purposes and promises. So each session ends with an opportunity to review the truths and challenges highlighted by the Bible study, and turn them into prayers of request and thanksgiving.

The **Leader's Guide** and introduction provide historical background information, explanations of the Bible texts for each session, ideas for **optional extra** activities, and guidance on how best to help people uncover the truths of God's word.

Why study 1 Thessalonians?

They tell how you turned to God from idols to serve the living and true God, and to wait for his Son from heaven, whom he raised from the dead—Jesus, who rescues us from the coming wrath. 1 Thessalonians 1 v 9-10

When a group of first-century pagans in the Greek city of Thessalonica first believed in Jesus, it was no small thing for them. They rejected the idols they had previously served, and were so transformed that they quickly became the talk of the ancient world—and a shining example for followers of Christ in the 20 centuries that have passed since then. They became known not only for what they rejected, but also for their faith, hope and love.

Do you feel like an ordinary Christian? Not especially gifted or knowledgeable? Does anyone really notice your faith? Does any of it matter? Then take time to look at the Thessalonian believers with this easy-to-follow guide.

The apostle Paul, thrilled to see their vibrant Christian lives, recorded his delight in this warm letter, packed with advice and encouragement to keep going. This was a transformation that would change lives, cultures and destinies far beyond ancient Macedonia.

Learn through this Good Book Guide how an unremarkable, pointless existence, can be transformed into a life marked by unshakeable faith, overflowing love and sensational hope. It is this kind of life that ordinary Christians like you are called to; so that, in our world of suffering, hostility and trials, we will be blameless and holy when our Lord Jesus comes.

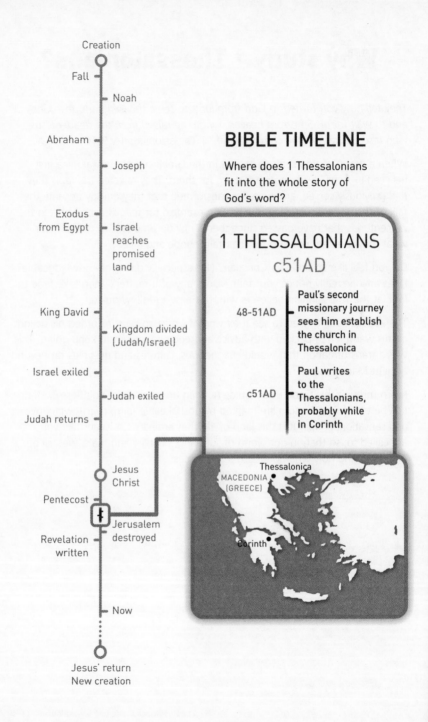

Creation
Fall
Noah
Abraham
Joseph
Exodus from Egypt
Israel reaches promised land
King David
Kingdom divided (Judah/Israel)
Israel exiled
Judah exiled
Judah returns
Jesus Christ
Pentecost
Jerusalem destroyed
Revelation written
Now
Jesus' return
New creation

BIBLE TIMELINE

Where does 1 Thessalonians fit into the whole story of God's word?

1 THESSALONIANS
c51AD

48-51AD | Paul's second missionary journey sees him establish the church in Thessalonica

c51AD | Paul writes to the Thessalonians, probably while in Corinth

Thessalonica
MACEDONIA (GREECE)
Corinth

1 Thessalonians overview
CHRISTIAN ENCOURAGEMENT

⊕ talkabout

1. How can other people best help you when you are attempting something difficult (for example a diet, an exam, breaking a bad habit)?

⊙ investigate

Paul had visited Thessalonica with Silas in about 50AD, and his preaching had resulted in the beginnings of a Christian church in the town. He had only been there for about three weeks, however, when he was forced to flee because of a riot (you can read the details of the story in Acts 17 v 1-9). This letter, one of the earliest of the New Testament letters, was written to the young church he had been forced to leave behind.

We're going to start by reading through the whole letter (it will only take about 15 minutes).

▶ Read 1 Thessalonians 1 v 1 – 5 v 28

2. How had the church in Thessalonica been getting on in Paul's absence?

3. How would you describe the relationship between Paul and the Thessalonians?

4. What specific issues does Paul deal with in this letter?

5. Paul's letter would originally have been read out loud (5 v 27). What encouragement do you imagine the original hearers would have received from these words?

⊡ **explore more**

optional

The encouragement of other Christians is an important theme throughout the New Testament letters. How do the following verses help explain further what Christian encouragement involves?

- *Ephesians 4 v 29*
- *Colossians 3 v 16*
- *Hebrews 10 v 24-25*

➔ **apply**

6. What similarities can you see between the church of the Thessalonians and your own church?

• What good things in this letter can you thank God for in your own church?

• What examples or instructions in this letter are a challenge to you and your church?

7.   Imagine a non-Christian friend discovers you are spending some time studying 1 Thessalonians. Having now read it all the way through, how might you begin to explain to them what the letter is all about?

• What can we learn about the good news of Jesus Christ?

• What can we learn about what it means to be a Christian?

What can we learn about the church—its work and its relationships?

⊡ getting personal

What are you looking forward to as you study 1 Thessalonians? Learning some first-century history, or having your heart, mind, and life changed by the living word of God? If God is speaking through these Bible studies, how can you make sure that you will hear and act upon what he says?

⊞ pray

Thank God:

• for the privilege of studying his word.

• for the encouragement we can receive from other Christians.

• for the joy of discovering God's will for our lives in the Scriptures.

Confess to God:

• ways in which you are not growing as you should be.

• times when you have not encouraged other Christians as you should have.

Ask God:

• for his blessing as you study 1 Thessalonians.

• for encouragement from his word for your day-to-day Christian living.

• for opportunities to encourage others.

• for the Spirit's help in putting these lessons into practice.

2

1 Thessalonians 1 v 1-10
WHAT A DIFFERENCE

The story so far

In 1 Thessalonians, Paul encourages believers to keep living a life of faith, love and hope.

talkabout

1. Discuss with a partner what people think of when they hear the word "Christian"? Ideally, what would you want them to think?

⊕ investigate

The church in Thessalonica was probably only months old when Paul wrote this letter, and yet there had been a radical change in the lives of the Christians there. Paul had heard reports that caused him to give thanks to God...

> **Read 1 Thessalonians 1 v 1-3**

2. How does Paul describe his readers in v 1?

DICTIONARY
Grace (v 1): an undeserved gift, freely given. **Faith (v 3):** belief and trust in God. **Labour (v 3):** work.

3. Paul speaks of his thankfulness in v 2. Why is he so thankful to God?

4. How does Paul know that these Christians have faith, love and hope?

⤷ apply

5. What practical difference does the good news about Jesus make to the lives of people who become Christians?

- "Your work produced by faith, your labour prompted by love and your endurance inspired by hope in our Lord Jesus Christ." What do these statements tell us about Christian faith, love and hope?

- Can you think of examples in your experience where Christian faith, love and hope have made a practical difference to the way someone lives?

⊡ **getting personal**

What practical difference has the good news about Jesus Christ made to your life? How would someone now looking at your life know that you are a Christian?

6. How can Paul's attitude to the Thessalonians encourage you in your attitude to your own church?

• Any truly Christian church is "in" God the Father and the Lord Jesus Christ (v 1). How does this make you respond?

⊡ **getting personal**

How recently have you thanked God for the fruits of faith, love and hope seen in your church?

⊙ **investigate**

▶ **Read 1 Thessalonians 1 v 4-10**

7. Why is Paul confident that God has chosen the Thessalonians?

> **DICTIONARY**
>
> **Gospel (v 5):** good news about Jesus.
> **Coming wrath (v 10):** God's anger and punishment of sin.

8. What difference has the gospel (the truth about Jesus) made to this new church?

9. What, in particular, did the other believers notice?

10. How was it, do you think, that the Thessalonians became famous for their faith in God, not just their good deeds?

⊡ explore more

optional

Verse 6 tells us how the Thessalonian Christians imitated Paul and his friends. Notice how Paul imitated the Lord and instructed young Christians to imitate him (see 1 Corinthians 11 v 1; Philippians 4 v 9; 2 Thessalonians 3 v 7-9).

In what way is the Lord Jesus an example for us to imitate? (See Matthew 16 v 24; Matthew 20 v 25-28; John 13 v 13-15; John 15 v 12-13.)

How have you benefited from godly role models like this?

To what extent do you think you are a good role model for others?

➔ apply

11. What signs, based on this passage, would you look for in a person's life to help you identify whether someone is truly a Christian?

• Imagine a non-Christian friend asks you what difference the good news about Jesus makes to your life. How might you use the ideas in this passage to answer that question?

⊡ getting personal

How similar is your experience to that of the Thessalonian church?

From these verses, how can you be sure you are a Christian?

What do you find the greatest personal encouragement in this chapter?

Why not give thanks to God for this encouragement now?

⬆ pray

From the passage, write down two things to thank and praise God for, something you need to confess to God, and two things to ask for.

Thank God...

Confess to God...

Ask God...

3 1 Thessalonians 2 v 1-16
HOW TO PLEASE GOD: PART 1

The story so far

Paul encourages believers to keep living a life of faith, love and hope, which transform lives.

⊕ talkabout

1. What sort of person would people in your community view as a "successful" church leader? Who would they view as a "failure"?

⬇ investigate: a ministry that pleases God

Paul had been forced to leave Thessalonica in a hurry. In Acts 17, we read that the "Jews were jealous; so they rounded up some bad characters from the market-place, formed a mob and started a riot in the city". Paul must have feared that the Thessalonians would judge his work among them a failure. Even worse, if they decided his work had been a failure, they might think that the gospel which he taught was also a failure.

▶ Read 1 Thessalonians 2 v 1-12

2. "You know, brothers, that our visit to you was not without results" (v 1). How does Paul show this in v 2-12?

> **DICTIONARY**
>
> **Apostles of Christ (v 6):** men sent out as Jesus' representatives.
> **Holy, righteous and blameless (v 10):** living God's way.

3. What evidence is there in the passage that Paul aimed to please God, not people?

⤷ apply

4. We all have opportunities to share the message about Jesus. When this happens, how might we be tempted to "please people"?

- What practical steps could we take to make sure we "are not trying to please people but God"?

- Church leaders have a difficult task in carrying out their special responsibility to teach the message about Jesus. How can we support our church leaders in this?

⊡ getting personal

If you had to pick one thing from this passage that would help you to be better at pleasing God, what would it be?

⬇ investigate

5. What was the aim of Paul's work among the Thessalonians? How did he go about achieving it?

6. In what ways was Paul like a mother?

7. In what ways did Paul deal with the believers "as a father"?

➔ apply

8. Paul's character and work are still under attack today. How do these verses give you confidence in Paul?

⬇ investigate: a response that pleases God

> **❯ Read 1 Thessalonians 2 v 13-16**

9. How had the Thessalonians responded to Paul's work and teaching?

10. How do we know that the Thessalonian church was successful in pleasing God?

⊡ **explore more**

optional

Compare the experience of these believers (see v 14-16) with the words of Jesus in Matthew 5 v 11-12.

Why is this kind of suffering a sign of success for God's people?

How can the experience of Jesus encourage us when we suffer in this way (see Acts 4 v 27-28 and 1 Peter 2 v 21-24)?

→ **apply**

11. In what ways is church different from other businesses or organisations? Think over what you have learned about...

• aims

• relationships

• signs of success

• How can these verses help us to know what we should be doing when we meet together as church?

⊡ getting personal

Be honest: what are the real reasons you go to church?

What things do you talk about with other believers at church?

What do you expect from church?

Think about whether any of these things need to change, as a result of what you have learned this session?

⬆ pray

Thank God...

• for Paul, and countless others throughout history, who have been faithful in their hard work for the Lord Jesus.

• for any encouragement, comfort and urging you have received.

• for the word of God, which is at work in those who believe.

Confess to God...

• any desire to please people rather than God.

• any deception, laziness or harshness.

Ask God...

• to help those who teach the good news about Jesus today.

• to help those who hear the gospel, that it may be accepted as the word of God.

• to help you, and your Christian brothers and sisters, to live a life worthy of God.

4 1 Thessalonians 2 v 17 – 3 v 13
FAITH THAT WORKS

The story so far

Paul encouraged believers to keep living a life of faith, love and hope, which transform lives.

Paul says that God-pleasing ministry is the work of teaching God's word and caring for people in order to build them up in the Christian faith.

⊕ talkabout

1. What do people think of when they hear the word "love"? How do most people go about showing love to someone?

⊕ investigate: growing in love

Paul's critics in the first century sometimes accused him of being harsh or unloving. His critics in the twenty-first century often make a similar accusation. And yet, Paul's writing often shows an intense love for others and a deep concern for their welfare.

> ▶ **Read 1 Thessalonians 2 v 17 – 3 v 13**

2. Which words or phrases here show Paul's love for the Thessalonian Christians?

DICTIONARY

The tempter (v 5): Satan; the devil.
Earnestly (v 10): sincerely and seriously.

3. In 1 v 3, Paul wrote about "labour prompted by love". What did Paul do for the Thessalonians, motivated by his love for them?

4. What was Paul's loving goal for the Thessalonian believers?

⊟ apply

5. In 1 v 6, Paul wrote: "You became imitators of us and of the Lord". Think of specific examples of how Paul and Jesus showed love to people.

• How could you imitate these?

• Despite passages like this, Paul is often considered to be hard and unloving. How do people get Paul's love wrong?

⊡ getting personal

How is your love for other Christians seen?

Would you say that this love is growing, or shrinking? Why?

How can you make sure it grows?

⬇ investigate: growing in faith

The Thessalonians were first-century heroes of the faith. If you remember from 1 v 8, their faith—their trust in God's promises—had "become known everywhere". And yet, Paul is still concerned for them. He still feels the need to send Timothy "to strengthen and encourage you in your faith" (3 v 2).

6. What challenges to their faith does Paul mention in 3 v 1-5?

7. How does Paul respond to Timothy's encouraging report?

➡ apply

8. How important to you is it that other Christians grow in their faith? How should this priority be seen in our everyday life?

- How could we pray more effectively for ourselves and for others to grow in faith?

⊡ getting personal

What do you think are the greatest dangers to your faith?

How can this passage strengthen you at such times?

⊡ explore more

optional

Faith and love have been—and will continue to be—very important themes in 1 Thessalonians. What do we learn about love and faith from the following verses?

- *1 v 3*
- *1 v 8-10*
- *2 v 8*
- *4 v 9-10*
- *5 v 8*

The third important theme in the letter is hope, and in 1 v 3 and 5 v 8 the three themes come together. Why do Christians need hope, as well as faith and love?

↥ pray

Think through what you have learned about faith and love, as you spend time praying together. Think about God's faithful promises to us, enabling us to put our faith in him; and think about the love that we have received from Him, that shows us how to love others. Think about how love and faith are seen among God's people.

From the passage write down things to thank and praise God for, something you need to confess to God, and things to ask for.

Thank God...

Confess to God...

Ask God...

5 1 Thessalonians 4 v 1-12
HOW TO PLEASE GOD: PART 2

The story so far

Paul encouraged believers to keep living a life of faith, love and hope, which transform lives.

Paul says that God-pleasing ministry is the work of teaching God's word and caring for people in order to build them up in the Christian faith.

Christians should have two priorities: growing in faith and growing in love.

⊕ talkabout

1. Imagine a survey which asks you to describe the sort of life that pleases God—what answers would people give? Which do you agree with?

⊙ investigate

Only the Christian life can be pleasing to God, because "without faith it is impossible to please him" (Hebrews 11 v 6). The Thessalonians were only able to "live in order to please God" once they had become "brothers" (v 1). However, having turned to God from idols, the Thessalonians received instruction from Paul on how to please God "more and more".

> **▶ Read 1 Thessalonians 4 v 1-12**

2. How have the Thessalonians been living? What does Paul urge them to do now?

DICTIONARY

Sanctified (v 3): set apart for God.
Pagans (v 5): non-believers.

3. Why does Paul's teaching on this subject of pleasing God carry such weight?

4. From these verses, summarise what holiness means in everyday life.

• v 3-8

• v 9-12

To be holy means to be set apart, to be different. God is holy, and he wants his people to be holy. Christians should have a lifestyle that is noticeably different from the lifestyle of non-Christians around them. This will be seen especially in sexual matters (v 3-8) and in social matters (v 9-12).

⊡ **explore more**

optional

What do the following verses teach about holiness?

Galatians 5 v 16-26: *What two groups of people are contrasted? How are Christians made holy? What part do Christians themselves play in becoming more holy?*

1 Peter 2 v 4-12: *What two groups of people are contrasted? What will Christians achieve through living holy lives?*

5. From v 3-8, how are Christians to avoid sexual immorality?

6. From v 3-8, how should the lives of Christians be seen to be different from the lives of non-Christians?

➔ apply

7. Paul claims the Lord's authority for his teaching (v 2 and 8) ie: these instructions are non-negotiable. But this teaching is under attack in the church today. How could you respond to people who say:

- "It's just too difficult to limit myself to sex only with my partner, only when I'm married."?

- "If you're hungry, you eat. If your body needs sex, you have sex. That's how God has made us, so what's the problem?"

- "Christianity is about freedom and forgiveness, not rules and restrictions! Why are Christians always stopping other people's fun, and judging anyone who doesn't fit in with their rules?"

- "How can we expect people to be attracted to Christianity when our attitude to sex comes from the Victorian age?"

⊕ **investigate**

8. From v 9-12, what responsibility do Christians have towards one another?

9. From v 9-12, how should the lives of Christians be seen to be different
from the lives of non-Christians?

⊟ **apply**

10. The Thessalonian believers were already living to please God (v 1). Why,
then, is Paul urging Christians to grow in godliness? Why do churches and
Christians need this kind of encouragement?

• When is this kind of encouragement needed? How will this affect
church activities and programmes?

- If a Christian friend, facing an important decision, comes to you and explains that they are seeking God's will for their life, how might you use these verses to help them make the right decision?

⬆ pray

Thank God...

- for the privilege of knowing how to please him.

- for the gift of the Holy Spirit, who helps us lead holy lives.

Confess to God...

- failures such as a lack of sexual self-control, wronging other Christians in sexual matters, not caring for fellow Christians or failing to lead a life that wins the respect of outsiders.

Ask God...

- to help you live a life of more and more holiness that pleases him.

- to help those who struggle to live holy lives.

- to help those who already seem to be model Christians.

6

1 Thessalonians 4 v 13 – 5 v 11

HOPE THAT INSPIRES

The story so far

Paul says that God-pleasing ministry is the work of teaching God's word and caring for people in order to build them up in the Christian faith.

Christians should have two priorities: growing in faith and growing in love.

God's will is that his people should live holy lives.

⊕ talkabout

1. What beliefs do people have in the face of death? Discuss how these beliefs affect the way they live?

Ever since Jesus returned to heaven, Christians have been waiting for him to come back. Of course, many Christians have died without having seen him. This fact appears to have troubled the Thessalonians, who presumably feared that their dead Christian friends would miss out. Many Christians still fear death and its implications today...

⊕ investigate: hope in the face of death

❯ Read 1 Thessalonians 4 v 13-18

2. Why don't Christians need to grieve "like the rest of mankind"?

3. According to these verses, what hope do Christians have in the face of death?

4. How does hope in Christ inspire us to endure as Christians (see 1 v 3)?

➔ **apply**

5. How might you "encourage one another with these words" (v 18)? Think of practical ays of doing this day by day.

• How do these verses help...

as you reflect on the death of a Christian friend?

as you pray for a sick Christian?

as you help a Christian who is being tempted or pressured to give up their faith?

⊡ getting personal

If you are a Christian, how do these verses inspire you to keep going?

Do you have a story of how this hope has helped you, in a time of difficulty, to stick at believing? Or have you seen this happen in someone else's life?

How can you make sure you never lose sight of this fantastic future?

⊕ investigate: hope in the face of wrath

The day of the Lord has been promised by Old Testament prophets. For some, it will be a terrible day of judgment; for others, it will be a wonderful day of victory and reward for all that has been suffered in this life. On that day, God's wrath will be seen as his anger burns against his enemies. In these next verses, Paul explains that the day of the Lord will be unannounced ("like a thief in the night"), it will be sudden ("while people are saying 'Peace and safety'"), and it is inevitable ("as labour pains on a pregnant woman").

❯ Read 1 Thessalonians 5 v 1-11

6. What does it mean to be a child "of the light" (v 5)? (Compare the words of Jesus in John 3 v 16-19.)

7. As children of the light, Christians should not be like everybody else, for we know this day is coming. How should we prepare for it?

8. What is the reason for Christian hope in the face of God's wrath (see also 1 v 10)?

⊡ **explore more**

optional

Read the following passages, and consider how the Old Testament prophets encouraged the people to prepare for the day of the Lord?

- *Isaiah 2 v 22*
- *Joel 2 v 12-14*
- *Zephaniah 1 v 7*

⊟ **apply**

9. How do these verses inspire you to keep going as a Christian... when you become discouraged or weary in doing good?

when you find it hard to talk to people about the Christian message?

when money, comfort or leisure distracts you from the Christian faith?

10. Are you alarmed by the thought of the day of the Lord? Why / why not?

* How will you "encourage one another and build each other up" this week?

⬆ pray

From the passage write down one thing to thank and praise God for, something you need to confess to God, and one thing to ask for.

Thank God...

Confess to God...

Ask God...

7 1 Thessalonians 5 v 12-28
FAITH, LOVE AND HOPE

The story so far

Paul says that God-pleasing ministry is the work of teaching God's word and caring for people in order to build them up in the Christian faith.

Christians should have two priorities: growing in faith and growing in love. God's will is that his people should live holy lives.

Knowing the truth about Jesus' return inspires Christians to endure.

⊕ talkabout

1. What does the average person in the street think goes on in church? Make a list together of the key things you would tell them about church.

⊕ investigate: love for God's people

The themes of faith, love and hope have dominated this letter.

• They are the hallmarks of authentic Christian living (1 v 3).

• Growing in them is a sign of Christian maturity (chapters 2 – 4).

• Living a life of faith, love and hope is the way to prepare for the return of the Lord Jesus Christ (5 v 8).

It is no surprise, therefore, that Paul closes his letter by encouraging the Thessalonians to have love for God's people, faith in God's provision, and hope in God's promises.

▸ Read 1 Thessalonians 5 v 12-15

2. How should Christians love their leaders?

3. How should Christians love their fellow Christians?

⊟ apply

4. What are some of the reasons why Christians fail to acknowledge/respect their leaders?

- How will a life of Christian faith, love and hope enable us to follow Paul's instructions here?

⊡ getting personal

What differences might you need to make in your approach to your church leaders?

5. What are some of the reasons why Christians fail to treat fellow Christians as Paul instructs?

• How will a life of Christian faith, love and hope enable us to do this?

☺ **getting personal**

From this passage, think of three specific ways in which you could better love other Christians. Be as practical and personal as possible!

1.

2.

3.

⊕ **investigate: faith in God's provision**

▶ **Read 1 Thessalonians 5 v 16-22**

6. From v 16-18, how should our faith in God's provision show itself?

7. As well as daily needs, God provides for our greatest need—that we might know him. He does this through the sword of the Spirit, which is the word of God. How should we show our faith in God's provision for our spiritual needs through his word?

➔ apply

8. How does the joyfulness, prayerfulness and thankfulness of Christians show their true faith in God?

• What helpful hints are given here to indicate what Christians should do when they meet together as church?

⊡ getting personal

When do you find it most difficult to have faith in God's provision? How do these verses help you?

⊥ investigate: hope in God's promises

❯ Read 1 Thessalonians 5 v 23-24

9. What will God do?

Sanctify (v 23): free from sin; set apart for God.

10. Why can we be so confident that he will do it?

⊖ apply

11. How do these two verses inspire you to keep going as a Christian?

⊥ investigate: conclusion

❯ Read 1 Thessalonians 5 v 25-28

12. What impact do you imagine the reading of this letter would have had?

Holy kiss (v 26): a common greeting; equivalent of a handshake.

⮕ apply

13. What impact has studying this letter had on you?

⬆ pray

From the whole letter, write down three things to thank and praise God for, something you need to confess to God, and three things to ask for.

Thank God...

Confess to God...

Ask God...

Living to please God

LEADER'S GUIDE

Leader's Guide

INTRODUCTION

Leading a Bible study can be a bit like herding cats—everyone has a different idea of what the passage could be about, and a different line of enquiry that they want to pursue. But a good group leader is more than someone who just referees this kind of discussion. You will want to:

- correctly understand and handle the Bible passage. But also...

- encourage and train the people in your group to do this for themselves. Don't fall into the trap of spoon-feeding people by simply passing on the information in the Leader's Guide. Then...

- make sure that no Bible study is finished without everyone knowing how the passage is relevant for them. What changes do you all need to make in the light of the things you have been learning? And finally...

- encourage the group to turn all that has been learned and discussed into prayer.

Your Bible-study group is unique, and you are likely to know better than anyone the capabilities, backgrounds and circumstances of the people you are leading. That's why we've designed these guides with a number of optional features. If they're a quiet bunch, you might want to spend longer on talkabout. If your time is limited, you can choose to skip explore more, or get people to look at these questions at home. Can't get enough of Bible study? Well, some studies have optional extra homework projects. As leader, you can adapt and select the material to the needs of your particular group.

So what's in the Leader's Guide?

The main thing that this Leader's Guide will help you to do is to understand the major teaching points in the passage you are studying, and how to apply them. As well as guidance on the questions, the Leader's Guide for each session contains the following important sections:

THE BIG IDEA

One or two key sentences will give you the main point of the session. This is what you should be aiming to have fixed in people's minds as they leave the Bible study. And it's the point you need to head back towards when the discussion goes off at a tangent.

SUMMARY

An overview of the passage, including plenty of useful historical background information.

OPTIONAL EXTRA

Usually this is an introductory activity that ties in with the main theme of the Bible study, and is designed to "break the ice" at the beginning of a session. Or it may be a "homework project" that people can tackle during the week.

So let's take a look at the various different features of a Good Book Guide:

⊕ talkabout

Each session kicks off with a discussion question, based on the group's opinions or experiences. It's designed to get people talking and thinking in a general way about the main subject of the Bible study.

⊡ investigate

The first thing you and your group need to know is what the Bible passage is about, which is the purpose of these questions. But watch out—people may come up with answers based on their experiences or teaching they have heard in the past, without referring to the passage at all. It's amazing how often we can get through a Bible study without actually looking at the Bible! If you're stuck for an answer, the Leader's Guide contains guidance on questions. These are the answers to direct your group to. This information isn't meant to be read out to people—ideally, you want them to discover these answers from the Bible for themselves. Sometimes there are optional follow-up questions (see ⊻ in guidance on questions) to help you help your group get to the answer.

⊡ explore more

These questions generally point people to other relevant parts of the Bible. They are useful for helping your group to see how the passage fits into the "big picture" of the whole Bible. These sections are OPTIONAL—only use them if you have time. Remember that it's better to finish in good time having really grasped one big thing from the passage, than to try and cram everything in.

→ apply

We want to encourage you to spend more time working at application—too often, it is simply tacked on at the end. In the Good Book Guides, apply sections are mixed in with the investigate sections of the study. We hope that people will realise that application is not just an optional extra, but rather, the whole purpose of studying the

Bible. We do Bible study so that our lives can be changed by what we hear from God's word. If you skip the application, the Bible study hasn't achieved its purpose.

These questions draw out practical lessons that we can all learn from the Bible passage. You can review what has been learned so far, and think about practical differences that this should make in our churches and our lives. The group gets the opportunity to talk about what they personally have learned.

⊡ getting personal

These can be done at home, but it is well worth allowing a few moments of quiet reflection during the study for each person to think and pray about specific changes they need to make in their own lives. Why not have a time for reporting back at the beginning of the following session, so that everyone can be encouraged and challenged by one another to make application a priority?

↑ pray

In Acts 4 v 25-30 the first Christians quoted Psalm 2 as they prayed in response to the persecution of the apostles by the Jewish religious leaders. Today however, it's not as common for Christians to base prayers on the truths of God's word as it once was. As a result, our prayers tend to be weak, superficial and self-centred rather than bold, visionary and God-centred.

The prayer section is based on what has been learned from the Bible passage. How different our prayer times would be if we were genuinely responding to what God has said to us through his word.

1

1 Thessalonians overview
CHRISTIAN ENCOURAGEMENT

THE BIG IDEA
Keep living a life of faith, love and hope, more and more.

SUMMARY
Paul writes to encourage the Thessalonian Christians to live to please God "more and more" (see especially 4 v 1). He is delighted by reports of their faith, love and hope (eg: 1 v 3), as these show that they are already living for God (eg: 1 v 9-10). He longs now that he might help them to continue to grow in Christian maturity (eg: 3 v 10).

GUIDANCE FOR QUESTIONS
1. How can other people best help you when you are attempting something difficult (for example a diet, an exam, breaking a bad habit)? Situations could range from following a diet to living the Christian life. Ideas might include personal conversations, letters and prayers, sharing similar experiences, reminding people about final outcomes and goals etc.

2. How had the church in Thessalonica been getting on in Paul's absence? The church's faith, love and hope were bearing fruit (1 v 3). They had become a model church (1 v 7) and their faith was widely known (1 v 8). They were facing trials (3 v 3) and temptations (3 v 5), but Timothy was able to report good news (3 v 6). Paul longed, however, that they might continue to grow in faith (3 v 10), love (3 v 12), holiness (4 v 1) and hope (4 v 13).

3. How would you describe the relationship between Paul and the Thessalonians? Paul was thankful (1 v 2) and joyful (3 v 8-9) because of their Christian growth. He had worked hard among them (2 v 9) and remained very close to them (2 v 17). He urged them (4 v 1) to live a holy life more and more. This is a letter of great personal warmth, written to much-loved Christian friends, encouraging them in faith, love and hope.

4. What specific issues does Paul deal with in this letter? Paul's three dominant themes are faith, love and hope (1 v 3 and 5 v 8). In light of these, he touches on the nature of conversion (chapter 1), the nature of Christian ministry (chapter 2), the faith and love of the Thessalonians (chapter 3), holiness (chapter 4), and the Christian hope (chapters 4 and 5).

5. Paul's letter would originally have been read out loud (5 v 27). What encouragement do you imagine the original hearers would have received from these words? It would have been good to be reassured of Paul's concern for their church; they would have been encouraged by his joy in their growth and challenged by his urging them to continue to grow and live more and more holy lives.

EXPLORE MORE
The encouragement of other Christians is an important theme throughout the New Testament letters. How do the following verses help explain further

what Christian encouragement involves?
Ephesians 4 v 29: The words we use are very important, and we should only say things which will build up other believers, according to their needs. Consider what needs other believers might have, and how our words could help build them up.
Colossians 3 v 16: "Let the message of Christ dwell among you richly as you teach and admonish one another with all wisdom." A follow-up question could consider the place of Scripture in teaching and admonishing one another.
Hebrews 10 v 24-25: Do not give up meeting together, but—with the day of Jesus' return approaching—encourage and spur one another on in godly living.

6. APPLY: What similarities can you see between the church of the Thessalonians and your own church?
All churches face the same challenges: to grow in faith, love and hope. All churches need the same help: the instructions of Scripture, the power of the Holy Spirit and the encouragement, support and prayers of fellow believers.

• **What good things in this letter can you thank God for in your own church?** See next question below.

• **What examples or instructions in this letter are a challenge to you and your church?** Discussions about your church can easily descend into grumbling and criticism, so the aim of these subsidiary questions is to focus everyone on positive reasons for thankfulness and practical responses to what is learned. Avoid discussing everything in detail—just share people's first impressions of the main lessons and encouragements in this letter.

7. APPLY: How might you begin to explain to a non-Christian friend what 1 Thessalonians is all about?
An encouragement to these Christians to go on living a life of faith, love and hope—for that is pleasing to God.

• **What can we learn about the good news of Jesus Christ?** The good news is that Jesus, the Son of God, rescues us from the coming wrath of God (1 v 10). He has saved us by dying for us (5 v 9-10), but God raised him back to life (4 v 14) and he is coming back again (1 v 10). At that time, he will punish people who have not lived to please God (4 v 6), but his people who have already died physically will be resurrected, and with all other Christians will live with Jesus for ever (4 v 14-17).

• **What can we learn about what it means to be a Christian?** A Christian is someone who has turned from idols to serve the living God, and wait for Jesus' return (1 v 9-10). A Christian lives a life that is shaped by faith, love and hope (1 v 3), and aims to please God in everything (4 v 1).

• **What can we learn about the church— its work and its relationships?** The church is a family of God's people (2 v 7, 11, 14 etc.), who teach the message about Jesus (2 v 4), who put it into practice in their own lives (2 v 13), and who encourage each other to continue in the faith (4 v 18; 5 v 11).

2 1 Thessalonians 1 v 1-10
WHAT A DIFFERENCE

THE BIG IDEA
The gospel brings faith, hope and love, which transform lives.

SUMMARY
Paul is thankful to God for the way in which the Thessalonians have responded to the gospel. The gospel which Paul proclaimed has changed their lives: their faith, love and hope can be seen in their lifestyle (v 3); having modelled themselves on Paul and Jesus (v 6), they are now in turn models for others (v 7); and their turning, serving and waiting is widely reported (v 9-10).

OPTIONAL EXTRA
Ask each group member to identify one older Christian who has been a godly role model (perhaps restrict the group's choices to those not in the room at the time!), and explain why they were so helpful. Then give thanks to God for these people.

GUIDANCE FOR QUESTIONS
1. Discuss with a partner what people think of when they hear the word "Christian"? Ideally, what would you want them to think? The purpose of this question is to air some commonly-held views of what a Christian is (eg: someone who believes in God, goes to church, a hypocrite etc), and then allow the teaching of the passage to reveal why these are inadequate ideas, or just plain wrong.

2. How does Paul describe his readers in v 1? They are a "church" (literally, a "gathering"), and they are "in" God the Father and the Lord Jesus Christ.

3. Paul speaks of his thankfulness in v 2. Why is he so thankful to God? God has brought the Thessalonian church into being through the gospel, and has protected it in Paul's absence. The changed lives of the Thessalonians are a work of God's grace.

4. How does Paul know that these Christians have faith, love and hope? Faith, love and hope have made a visible difference to the lives of the Thessalonian believers. These things can be seen by what these Christians actually do. Because of their faith, hope and love they work, labour and endure (v 3).

5. APPLY: What practical difference does the good news about Jesus make to the lives of people who become Christians? Allow people to discuss the practical changes they have seen, or expect to see, in the lives of those who become Christians, but also guide them to the answer found in the passage: they work and labour because of their faith and love, and they keep going as Christians through difficult times because of their hope. It means nothing to say we have faith, love or hope if the way we live has not changed.

- **"Your work produced by faith, your labour produced by love and your endurance inspired by hope in our Lord Jesus Christ." What do these statements tell us about Christian faith, love and hope?**
- **Faith:** If we trust God's promises (ie: have faith), we will act and work accordingly—we will be joyful, we will be prayerful, we will be thankful (see 5 v 16-18). You could ask the follow-up question: What kind of

work is produced by faith?

- **Love:** Our love for God and our love for others will be shown in our actions—we will be focused on the needs of others, we will be willing to be deprived for others, and our life will be wrapped up in the well-being of others (see Paul in 3 v 1-13).

- **Hope:** We have a hope for the future which means we persevere in the present. Believing that Jesus will return and take us to be with him (4 v 13-18) inspires us to endure any sufferings we may face now.

- **Can you think of examples in your experience where Christian faith, love and hope have made a practical difference to the way someone lives?** Don't be scared of silence. Give people time to come up with examples that they have noticed.

6. APPLY: How can Paul's attitude to the Thessalonians encourage you in your attitude to your own church? Paul's attitude towards the Thessalonian believers is, first and foremost, one of thankfulness to God for the evidence of their faith that he has seen in their lives.

☒

- **Why was Paul so thankful for other Christians, and why are we so often not thankful?** Perhaps this indicates that we have different priorities from Paul eg: expecting to benefit from other Christians rather than serving them by building them up in Christ, focused on our social life rather than the gospel etc.

- **Any truly Christian church is "in" God the Father and the Lord Jesus Christ (v 1). How does this make you respond?** Perhaps this should help us to respond with confidence, closeness, joy…

7. Why is Paul confident that God has chosen the Thessalonians? v 4-5: The effect of the gospel in their lives is proof that God has chosen them to be his people. Paul is not implying here that sometimes the gospel comes merely with words, whereas at other times it comes with power, the Holy Spirit and deep conviction. Rather, the Spirit of God takes the word of God (the gospel in spoken form) and brings it to those God has chosen to save with power and conviction— an irresistible combination!

8. What difference has the gospel (the truth about Jesus) made to this new church? They welcomed the message with the Spirit's joy (v 6); as well as being imitators (v 6), they were imitated (v 7); the message "rang out" from them (v 8) as they turned to God from idols (v 9), to serve (v 9) and to wait for Jesus' return (v 10).

9. What, in particular, did the other believers notice? Their faith in God (v 8).

☒

- **How would their faith have become known?** Presumably through the work it produced—v 3.

10. How was it, do you think, that the Thessalonians became famous for their faith in God, not just their good deeds? Although the faith of the Thessalonian believers is recognised by the kind of lives that they lived, it is identified as "faith in God", not just good deeds. Notice also v 8—"The Lord's message rang out from you". This shows us that part of the work and labour produced by Christian faith and love involves communicating the truth about Jesus. The challenge for us is that if we simply do good things, without any explanation of why we are doing good, nobody will know about our faith in God.

EXPLORE MORE
In what way is the Lord Jesus an example for us to imitate?
Matthew 16 v 24: By denying ourselves and taking up our cross: putting to death our own interests and desires in the service of God.
Matthew 20 v 25-28: By serving others rather than expecting to be served by them.
John 13 v 13-15: By "washing one another's feet"—humbling ourselves in the service of others, instead of seeking recognition and honour for our service.
John 15 v 12-13: Loving others by being ready to lay down our lives.
How have you benefited from godly role models like this? To what extent do you think you are a good role model for others? Notice how Paul repeatedly instructs young Christians to imitate him, just as he imitates Christ (1 Corinthians 11 v 1); in everything they have learned, received and heard from, or seen in him (Philippians 4 v 9); in his hard work for them (2 Thessalonians 3 v 7-9). When discussing role models, be prepared to assess the positive and the negative aspects! Most of us will be role models for others, perhaps unwittingly.

⊻
- **In what ways are we helpful in this regard?**
- **In what ways might we be unhelpful?**

11. APPLY: What signs, based on this passage, would you look for in a person's life to help you identify whether someone is truly a Christian?
Examples given in the passage include:
- receiving Christian teaching positively—v 9 (both the written word of God and biblical teachers).
- turning from idols—v 9 (discuss what this looks like).
- serving God—v 9 (discuss how we do this).
- waiting for Jesus—v 10, which is not simply doing nothing (see 4 v 18 and 5 v 11 for the practical implications of this).

- **Imagine a non-Christian friend asks you what difference the good news about Jesus makes to your life. How might you use the ideas in this passage to answer that question?** You could summarise under the headings of turning, serving and waiting in v 9-10. This could be an opportunity for brief encouragement in personal evangelism.

3 1 Thessalonians 2 v 1-16
HOW TO PLEASE GOD: PART 1

THE BIG IDEA
This passage shows us what God-pleasing ministry looks like. "Ministry" = the work of teaching God's word and caring for people in order to build them up in their faith.

OPTIONAL EXTRA
Imagine that your church is looking for a new home/small/fellowship group leader. What characteristics and qualities would you be looking for? (**Note:** please be kind and compassionate about existing group leaders—especially if they are within earshot!)

SUMMARY
Paul explains that his work among them was pleasing to God. He told people the gospel (v 2), he served God (v 4), he acted in holiness (v 10), and he dealt with people with tenderness (v 7, 11). The true nature of his work was recognised by the Thessalonian believers at the time—they received the message not as a human word, but as the word of God (v 13).

Note: It's important to remember that Paul was one of the apostles (1 Corinthians 15 v 3-10)—a small group of specially chosen men, who lived at the same time as Jesus, who had met and had been chosen by him, and whose job was to continue the work of Jesus Christ and lay the foundations of his church (Ephesians 2 v 20).

All of this means that there are no apostles in the church today—at least, not in the sense that Paul was an apostle. So, although there are many things in Paul's ministry and way of life that all Christians should imitate,

no Christian today can speak and act with Paul's apostolic authority (see 4 v 8 for an example of this). We can't become apostles like Paul, but we can learn from his life what Christian service is and how it should be carried out to please God.

GUIDANCE FOR QUESTIONS
1. What sort of person would people in your community view as a "successful" church leader? Who would they view as a "failure"? There may well be a wide variety of answers to this question. Try to avoid assessing each suggestion in too much depth—the Bible's answer will become increasingly clear during this session.

2. "You know, brothers, that our visit to you was not without results" (v 1). How does Paul show this in v 2-12? Paul measures success and failure not by (for example) popularity, but by faithfulness. He dared to tell them the gospel (v 2); he was a God-pleaser, not a people-pleaser (v 4); he was gentle (v 7), loving (v 8), hard-working (v 9) and holy (v 10); ultimately, he was urging them to live a life worthy of God (v 12).

3. What evidence is there in the passage that Paul aimed to please God, not people? Awareness that God tests hearts (v 4); no flattery or deception (v 5); not seeking praise from men (v 6); his priorities were God-centred, not man-centred (v 12).

4. APPLY: We all have opportunities to share the message about Jesus. When this happens, how might we be tempted to "please people"? We may be tempted in different ways: in what we say, decisions we take, the way we spend time, and the confrontations we shy away from.

• **What practical steps could we take to make sure we "are not trying to please people but God"?** Regularly reviewing and praying through Bible passages like verses 1-6 will help, as well as the support of faithful Christian friends.

• **Church leaders have a difficult task in carrying out their special responsibility to teach the message about Jesus. How can we support our church leaders in this?** We can all pray for our leaders and encourage them week by week, by listening to the teaching, responding actively and positively, thanking them and letting them know how the teaching has helped us, supporting them financially, helping out practically, showing our love for them by what we give or do for them etc. Some people (but not all!) may be in a position where it would be appropriate to offer accountability and/or positive criticism.

5. What was the aim of Paul's work among the Thessalonians? How did he go about achieving it? Paul's aim was for the Thessalonians "to live lives worthy of God" (v 12). To this end, he taught them the gospel (v 8), but in addition, he also cared for them (v 7), shared his life with them (v 8), became a role model for them (v 10), and encouraged them in various ways to put into practice the things that they had been taught (v 11-12).

6. In what ways was Paul like a mother? He was not a burden but gentle (v 7), he loved them so much that he shared his life with them (v 8), and he worked hard night and day (v 9).

7. In what ways did Paul deal with the believers "as a father"? He encouraged, comforted and urged them to live lives worthy of God (v 12).

• How do encouraging, comforting and urging differ from, and complement, one another?

8. APPLY: Paul's character and work are still under attack today. How do these verses give you confidence in Paul? Paul's ministry was authentic and his godliness genuine, so whatever attacks may be made on his ministry (eg: with regard to homosexuality or the role of women), we can be confident that he taught the truth without personal malice or prejudice.

9. How had the Thessalonians responded to Paul's work and teaching? They had accepted Paul's message as the word of God (v 13) which was now at work in them. As a result, they were able to cope with the trials and sufferings they were facing. Don't spend too much time on the issues surrounding the Jews in v 14-16; they are a secondary issue in Paul's argument. The primary issue is that the Thessalonians' suffering is not unique. If people in the group are concerned that Paul is being anti-Semitic, Romans 9 v 1-5 is helpful.

10. How do we know that the Thessalonian church was successful in pleasing God? Verses 14-15—the sign of their success was the fact that they were suffering in the same way as their Christian brothers and sisters, as had the prophets of God and the Lord Jesus himself, at the hands of those who were displeasing God.

EXPLORE MORE
Compare the experience of these believers (see v 14-16) with the words of Jesus in Matthew 5 v 11-12. Why is this kind of suffering a sign of success for God's people? Jesus warned that his followers would be unjustly persecuted because of their faithfulness to Jesus (v 11) and because of their faithfulness to God's word—"in the same way they persecuted the prophets" (v 12). That is, they would suffer because they were successful in pleasing God.
How can the experience of Jesus encourage us when we suffer in this way (see Acts 4 v 27-28 and 1 Peter 2 v 21-24)? In persecution, we can be encouraged by the fact that those who caused Jesus' suffering were being used by God to work out his sovereign plan (Acts 4 v 27-28). And the result of Jesus' suffering was our salvation (1 Peter 2 v 21-24). In the same way, the suffering of God's people is not a terrible mistake, and it achieves great good in God's plans and purposes.

11. APPLY: In what ways is church different from other businesses or organisations? Think over what you have learned about...
- **aims:** Church is different because we aim to please God, not people. The aim of church is to enable people to live lives worthy of God (v 12).
- **relationships:** Relationships are not distant, professional, utilitarian or exploitative. They are family relationships; notice the words Paul uses as he describes his relationship with these believers— brothers and sisters (v 1, 14), mother (v 7), father (v 11), children (v 11).
- **signs of success:** Success is faithfulness to the word of God, and a sign of success is persecution from those who displease God.
- **How can these verses help us to know what we should be doing when we meet together as church?** When we meet as church, we should be governed by the need for teaching the truth about Jesus, the need to care for one another, and the need to be encouraged to live holy lives.

4 1 Thessalonians 2 v 17 – 3 v 13
FAITH THAT WORKS

THE BIG IDEA
Two priorities for Christians: growing in faith and growing in love.

SUMMARY
Paul's concern was that the Thessalonians would grow in faith and love. Unable to be with them personally, he sent Timothy from Athens to find out how they were doing and to encourage them in their faith. Timothy's recent return (3 v 6), with the good news about their faith and love, causes Paul to rejoice. However, their faith is still lacking (v 10) and needs supplying, and their love (v 12) must increase and overflow.

GUIDANCE FOR QUESTIONS
1. What do people think of when they hear the word "love"? How do most people go about showing love to someone? Common views include: people have no control over who they love or don't love; love is romantic; love accepts people just as they are and doesn't try to change them; love is shown by physical affection; love makes people feel good about themselves; love does things that people enjoy, rather than things that they dislike.

2. Which words or phrases here show Paul's love for the Thessalonian Christians? A list could include the following: intense longing (2 v 17); "For what is our hope, our joy ... Is it not you?" (v 19); "We thank God ... in return for all the joy we have ... because of you" (3 v 9); "We pray most earnestly" (3 v 10); "May the Lord make your love increase and overflow ... just as ours does for you" (v 12).

3. In 1 v 3, Paul wrote about "labour prompted by love". What did Paul do for the Thessalonians, motivated by his love for them? Paul tried to come and see them (2 v 18); he sent Timothy to them (3 v 2); and he prayed most earnestly for them (v 10). Sending Timothy must have been particularly hard for Paul, as he would have missed Timothy's company during such a difficult time in Athens.

4. What was Paul's loving goal for the Thessalonian believers? Paul wanted them to "be blameless and holy in the presence of our God and Father when our Lord Jesus comes" (3 v 13). It was for this reason that he prayed and acted to make sure that they would stand firm in the Lord (v 8), and that he could supply what was lacking in their faith (v 10).

5. APPLY: In 1 v 6, Paul wrote: "You became imitators of us and of the Lord". Think of specific examples of how Paul and Jesus showed love to people. How could you imitate these?
Paul: prayer for others, constant encouragement, always thinking about their needs, watchful for anything that could harm their faith, sacrificing his own interests and comforts to serve them (eg: 3 v 2, 10)
Jesus: humility, service, compassion, refuting error, helping people admit their sinfulness, showing grief (eg: at Lazarus' grave), showing anger (eg: towards the Pharisees, in the temple) etc.
Allow your group to come up with examples and encourage practical suggestions about how we can imitate these examples.

- **Despite passages like this, Paul is often considered to be hard and unloving. How do people get Paul's love wrong?** The key to understanding Paul's love is his goal for the Thessalonians (3 v 13). People who do not have the same goal will not understand Paul's love. For instance, Paul shows his love by teaching that God will punish deliberate sexual immorality (4 v 6), because he knows that this way of life will destroy a person's faith, but this can seem unnecessarily harsh to people who do not share Paul's goal of producing Christians who will be blameless and holy when the Lord returns.

GETTING PERSONAL
How is your love for other Christians seen? The key is to move away from thinking about love in abstract terms, and to pin down specific ways in which our love is shown in everyday reality—eg: writing a letter to cheer someone up, helping with the cooking or babysitting, inviting others for meals, or praying for someone.
Would you say that this love is growing, or shrinking? Why? This is a question to encourage people to think about the state of their love for fellow Christians. It is rare that such love will remain static—it will either be growing or shrinking.

6. What challenges to their faith does Paul mention in 3 v 1-5? Paul mentions trials in v 3 and the tempter in v 5. Trials are those difficult times in life that unsettle us, not least by causing us to doubt God's goodness and faithfulness. The particular trial that Paul is speaking of here is persecution. The work of the tempter is to lead us astray through various temptations, so that we might abandon (or at least sideline) our love for Jesus and trust in the gospel.

7. How does Paul respond to Timothy's encouraging report? Paul is delighted (3 v 8), thanks God (v 9) and prays for them (v 10).

8. APPLY: How important to you is it that other Christians grow in their faith? This priority will be seen most clearly in our prayer life, but also in our conversations and our use of time. For most Christians, it is important that others grow in the faith—but this becomes only one priority among many (family, career, leisure) and can often be ignored.

- **How should this priority be seen in our everyday life?** Some ideas: daily prayer—who do we pray for and how? What about one phone call or e-mail a day to encourage others in their faith? How could we use our homes/cars/leisure activities for gospel work? If possible, how could we get the whole family involved?

- **How could we pray more effectively for ourselves and for others to grow in faith?** Perhaps use 3 v 12-13 as a basis for prayer. Some people find it helpful to have a prayer list or diary, in which they can write down the names of people to pray for and jot down answers to prayer as the months go by.

EXPLORE MORE
Faith and love have been—and will continue to be—very important themes in 1 Thessalonians. What do we learn about love and faith from the following verses?
- **1 v 3:** Faith and love are two of the three things for which Paul gives thanks, faith producing work and love prompting labour.
- **1 v 8-10:** Their faith is well known everywhere because they have turned to

God from idols to serve and wait.

- **2 v 8:** Paul loved them so much he was willing to share not only the gospel but also his life, despite the hard work this involved (2 v 9).
- **4 v 9-10:** The Thessalonians have a brotherly love for all the Macedonian brothers, but are urged to love them more and more.
- **5 v 8:** Faith and love are the breastplate to be put on in readiness for Jesus' return—in other words, putting into practice faith and love (along with hope) is the way in which Christians make themselves ready for the second coming of Jesus Christ.

The third important theme in the letter is hope, and in 1 v 3 and 5 v 8 the three themes come together. Why do Christians need hope, as well as faith and love? Hope inspires endurance (1 v 3), and without this endurance faith and love could easily die. Faith is what makes us look upwards to God, and love outwards to others, but hope is what keeps us going forward in faith and love.

OPTIONAL EXTRA

In *The Screwtape Letters*, CS Lewis wrote the imaginary letters of a senior devil to his young apprentice. In these letters, there is lots of advice on how the younger devil might tempt the young Christian in his "care", and cause him to give up the Christian life. What "devilish" advice might be given to cause you to stumble and fall? What steps could you take to counter these efforts, and grow in faith and love instead?

5 1 Thessalonians 4 v 1-12
HOW TO PLEASE GOD: PART 2

THE BIG IDEA
God's will is that his people should live holy lives.

SUMMARY
Paul had previously taught the Thessalonians how to please God. He acknowledges that they are living this way but now urges them to do so "more and more" (v 1), reminding them of the authority of his teaching (v 2, also v 8). He touches on both sexual matters (v 3-8) and social matters (v 9-12).

Note: As is often the case with Bible study, we deal with issues that are personal and sensitive. Great care will be needed, especially from the leader, when studying issues of sexuality, to ensure that the truth is spoken in love. This may give a great opportunity to once again tell the gospel and apply the message of repentance, forgiveness, assurance of salvation and eternal life.

OPTIONAL EXTRA
Distinctives by Vaughan Roberts is a very helpful short book on living a distinctively holy life. Perhaps each member of the group could read a different chapter during the week, and then report back on what they have read.

GUIDANCE FOR QUESTIONS
1. Imagine a survey which asks you to describe the sort of life that pleases God—what answers would people give? Which do you agree with?
Answers often include: obedience to the Ten Commandments / Sermon on the Mount; regular attendance at church; prayer; helping others etc. The underlying issue is to find out what people think will please God.

2. How have the Thessalonians been living? What does Paul urge them to do now? Paul is aware that the Thessalonian believers are already living holy lives, but he urges them now to do so more and more (v 1).

3. Why does Paul's teaching on this subject of pleasing God carry such weight? Paul's instructions have the authority of Jesus (v 2). Therefore, anyone who rejects this instruction is not rejecting Paul but God himself (v 8).

4. From these verses, summarise what holiness means in everyday life.
• **v 3-8:** Purity in sexual matters.
• **v 9-12:** Purity in social matters.

EXPLORE MORE
What do the following verses teach about holiness?
• **Galatians 5 v 16-26: What two groups of people are contrasted? How are Christians made holy? What part do Christians themselves play in becoming more holy?:** Those who live by the flesh / sinful nature (non-Christians) are contrasted with those who live by the Spirit (Christians). It is the Spirit who makes people able to live to please God. But Christians themselves "have crucified the flesh" (v 24) and must "keep in step with the Spirit" (v 25). In other words, the work of the Spirit in making someone holy is seen in the person's efforts to live a holy life.

- **1 Peter 2 v 4-12: What two groups of people are contrasted? What will Christians achieve through living holy lives?** Those who come to Jesus (v 4), trust in Him (v 6) and believe (v 7) are contrasted with those who do not believe (v 7), have rejected Jesus (v 7) and disobey the message (v 8)—just what the Christians that Peter was writing to were once like. It is holy people that are able to declare God's praises (v 9) and cause pagans to glorify God (v 12).

5. From v 3-8, how are Christians to avoid sexual immorality? Christians should have self-control, not self-indulgence (v 4), and should strive for holiness, not "pagan-ness" (v 5). In other words, we avoid sexual immorality by keeping a close rein on our own bodies (especially our sexuality), and by seeking to be different from people around us (holiness) rather than just like them ("pagan-ness").

6. From v 3-8, how should the lives of Christians be seen to be different from the lives of non-Christians? Christians should not be self-indulgent and lustful, and in this way will avoid wronging or taking advantage of others (v 6).

7. APPLY: Paul claims the Lord's authority for his teaching (v 2 and 8) ie: these instructions are non-negotiable. But this teaching is under attack in the church today. These verses instruct us to control ourselves and restrict our desires sexually, but the message of the world is completely opposite—in fact, self-restriction and control of our sexuality is often thought to be harmful. Some people today believe that Christians should change their thinking according to the world's understanding. But the underlying theme of these verses

is that Christians should be different from the world—holy). Be prepared to answer (at some point) questions on sex before marriage, co-habitation, adultery and homosexuality (1 Corinthians 6 v 12 – 7 v 40 may be helpful here).

How could you respond to people who say:
- **"It's just too difficult to limit myself to sex only with my partner, only when I'm married."?** There is no one to who holiness comes naturally. First we need to receive God's Spirit, ie: become a Christian. Then, when we live by the Spirit, he helps us to produce the fruit of the Spirit (eg: self-control), and to give up the acts of the sinful nature. It takes effort on our part to "keep in step with the Spirit" but with his help it is now possible to live a holy life.
- **"If you're hungry, you eat. If your body needs sex, you have sex. That's how God has made us, so what's the problem?"** God has made us, and, as our Creator, he knows what is best for us. He has given humans the gift of sex, and also instructions about how to use this gift. If we ignore his instructions, we will run into serious problems. Sexual desire is not the same as hunger—people starve without food but no one has ever died from lack of sex. The big question is: do we trust our Creator?
- **"Christianity is about freedom and forgiveness, not rules and restrictions! Why are Christians always stopping other people's fun, and judging anyone who doesn't fit in with their rules?"** Loads of misconceptions here! **Sex:** It isn't primarily for fun—it's the ultimate expression of intimacy and devotion between a man and a woman.

Sex without any binding commitment to love the other person for better or worse is simply using someone else's body for our own selfish gratification, and it's certainly not fun to be used in that way.

Freedom: It isn't an unrestricted ability to do whatever we want—that only leads us into becoming enslaved to our selfish desires.

Rules and restrictions: There's nothing necessarily wrong with them— life without rules is simply chaos, where only the strongest and most ruthless will get what they want, but God's rules free us to live to please him.

Forgiveness: It's not incompatible with personal holiness—Jesus is the ultimate example of holiness, yet he was loved most by "sinners" for the way in which he taught and practised forgiveness.

• **How can we expect people to be attracted to Christianity when our attitude to sex comes from the Victorian age?"** A biblical understanding of God's gift of sex is certainly not the same as the Victorian view of sex. Apart from this, the central issue for Christians is not attracting people to Christianity, but living to please God so that pagans will one day glorify him. We are told that Christians achieve this by living holy and good lives (1 Peter 2 v 12), which includes avoiding sexual immorality. Will we trust God or will we do what we think is best?

8. From v 9-12, what responsibility do Christians have towards one another? God teaches us to love one another (v 9) and not to place burdens on one another (v 11). By "mind your own business", Paul does not mean we should not be involved in the lives of others (eg: see 5 v 11 or 14-15—Paul's instructions to build one another up and warn individuals against particular sins) but that we should look out for our own affairs, rather than depending on others to help us out (v 12).

9. From v 9-12, how should the lives of Christians be seen to be different from the lives of non-Christians? A life of love and peace will win the respect of outsiders (v 12).

10. APPLY: The Thessalonian believers were already living to please God (v 1). Why, then, is Paul urging Christians to grow in godliness? Why do churches and Christians need this kind of encouragement? God gives us his Spirit (v 8), but we have a responsibility to keep in step with his Spirit by avoiding sexual immorality and loving one another. This is not easy, so we need constant reminders and urging. Use these follow-up questions to help your group answer this question.

⊡

• **What is Paul's goal for these Christians (3 v 13)?** That they will be blameless and holy when Jesus Christ returns.
• **What is Paul's fear for these Christians (3 v 5)?** That they will be tempted away from their faith.
• **What is Paul's desire for these Christians (3 v 10 and 12; 4 v 1 and 10)?** That they will increase in their faith (3 v 10), love (3 v 12, 4 v 10), and holiness (4 v 1).
• **How are these three things connected?** (It is only by living to please God "more and more" that Christians guard themselves against the danger of giving up their faith, and so are able to persevere in holy living until the return of Jesus Christ.

• **When is this kind of encouragement needed? How will this affect church activities and programmes?** Paul was encouraging these Christians to live holy lives at a time when they were already following his instructions. This kind of encouragement is needed even when Christians are doing well, not just when people have problems and are in danger of giving up. Churches need to look after strong Christians as well as struggling ones— eg: we should pray for them; leaders should spend time and give attention to them; they should be given opportunities to hear and discuss the teaching instead of always serving others in Sunday school, youth ministry, crèche.

• **If a Christian friend, facing an important decision, comes to you and explains that they are seeking God's will for their life, how might you use these verses to help them make the right decision?** God's will is that we be holy (v 3). In any particular situation, it is good to consider the following questions: How can I best be holy? How will this decision affect my sexual morality? How will this decision affect my ability to love other Christians?

1 Thessalonians 4 v 13 – 5 v 11

6 HOPE THAT INSPIRES

THE BIG IDEA
Knowing the truth about Jesus' return inspires Christians to endure.

SUMMARY
Christians believe that Jesus will return, and this hope inspires us to endure in two ways. Firstly, we need no longer fear death nor worry about those who have died "in Christ" (4 v 13-18). Secondly, we can be ready for him and so need not fear God's judgment (5 v 1-11). However, "ignorance" about these things causes unnecessary grief and pain, and being "in darkness" about Jesus' return means being in danger of destruction. Christians should therefore encourage each other with these truths, so we're confident in our hope (4 v 18; 5 v 11).

Note: Sadly, any Bible study on the return of the Lord Jesus runs the risk of being hijacked by a discussion of various ideas about the end of the world. This is especially the case here, as 4 v 17 is a key verse for one particular view ("the pre-millennial rapture"). Leaving aside the obvious point that there is insufficient evidence in this one passage to settle these debates, the real danger is that the main point of the study (being inspired to endure because of the hope we have in Jesus' return) will get forgotten. If possible, try to prevent great debates on "end of the world" theories, or the best interpretation of Daniel and Revelation, so as to leave time for a thorough study of these verses. If it can't be prevented, at least delay it until coffee!

OPTIONAL EXTRA

Imagine a member of your group is going to meet a friend who has just lost their Christian mother. What advice might you give them about what to say?

GUIDANCE FOR QUESTIONS

Note: It would be worth ensuring early on that people understand what is meant by our hope in Christ—namely, the hope and confidence we have because of what will happen when Jesus returns, as can be seen in this chapter. There can also be some slight confusion in this passage arising from Paul's use of "awake" and "asleep". Sometimes he refers to those who are alive or dead (as in 4 v 14 or 5 v 10); by contrast, in 5 v 6- 7, he refers to those who are spiritually awake or spiritually asleep. On each occasion, the context makes Paul's meaning clear.

1. What beliefs do people have in the face of death? Discuss how these beliefs affect the way they live? For example, if people believe that this life is all there is, they will be desperate to make the most of what they have now, regardless of the cost to others. Or, those who hope to get into heaven by faithfully following their religion can end up feeling permanently guilty and fiercely driven about complying with religious duties. The point is that what we believe about our destiny beyond the grave does affect how we live. Christians, who have a uniquely certain hope of eternal life, should be living in a way that is completely different from the rest of the world.

2. Why don't Christians need to grieve "like the rest of mankind"? We know that, for those who believe in Jesus, there is life after death. Although we will still mourn and grieve the loss of a fellow Christian, we are able to do so in the knowledge that

we will one day be reunited with them in Christ. The rest of mankind (non-Christians) do not have this comfort, and so they grieve without hope.

⊗

• **Why do you think Paul uses the term "fall asleep" for Christians (4 v 13, 15)?** (It tells us that the Christian experience of physical death is not actually death at all; it is as harmless for us as falling asleep and in the same way that we wake in the morning, we will rise to eternal life when Jesus returns.

3. According to these verses, what hope do Christians have in the face of death? Jesus has proved that there is a resurrection (v 14) by rising from the dead. Furthermore, he has promised by his own word (v 15 —possibly a reference to Matthew 24 v 31, or maybe an unrecorded saying of Jesus) that there is a resurrection both for those Christians who have already died (v 14 and 16) and those who are still alive on earth when he returns (v 17).

4. How does hope in Christ inspire us to endure as Christians (see 1 v 3)? Check that people understand how Paul uses the word "hope". He refers to a conviction about something that is certain, rather than a wish for something that is uncertain. Our hope in Christ is that he will return to take us to be with him in heaven for ever—this helps to put the troubles of this life into perspective, enabling us to endure whatever may happen in the short term. You may like to compare Hebrews 10 v 36-37 and 2 Corinthians 4 v 17 for the New Testament teaching on how Christians should view a life of difficulty and suffering in this world.

5. APPLY: How might you "encourage one another with these words" (v 18)? Think of practical ways of doing this day by day. Encourage the group to come up with practical ideas about the times and ways in which we can talk together about the resurrection, and seek comfort in Christian truth. Eg: Is this ever mentioned in prayers? What do you write on cards or emails to one another? As you read the Bible or hear teaching, do you ask yourself how you will use these truths to encourage Christians that you know?

• **How do these verses help...**
  ...as you reflect on the death of a Christian friend? Those who have died in Christ will not miss out and we will be caught up together with them to meet the Lord.
  ...as you pray for a sick Christian? Although there is nothing wrong with praying for healing, we need to recognise that ultimately "falling asleep" is by far the better option for a Christian brother or sister. So we can pray with confidence that whatever God chooses for that person will be good, rather than desperately seeking a miracle of healing, and suffering a crisis of faith if God does not do this.
  ...as you help a Christian who is being tempted or pressured to give up their faith? To give up our faith and live according to the world's godless agenda is to go through life as though drunk or asleep, as we head for inescapable destruction. On the other hand, if we persevere in our faith, we will look back on the troubles we experience as light and momentary, and see that they have achieved an eternal glory that far outweighs them all (2 Corinthians 4 v 17).

6. What does it mean to be a child "of the light" (v 5)? (Compare the words of Jesus in John 3 v 16-19.) Christians belong to the day, not the night, because they are enlightened and know that the day of the Lord is coming (v 4). But this phrase indicates more than simply having information that others do not have. Jesus' words in John 3 v 16-19 show that people come into the light by believing in "the Light" (Jesus)—ie: becoming a Christian. And what keeps people in darkness is not lack of knowledge but fear of their evil deeds being exposed, which causes them to suppress the truth they receive. In other words, only a Christian can be prepared for the day of the Lord.

7. As children of the light, Christians should not be like everybody else, for we know this day is coming. How should we prepare for it? We should be awake and sober (v 6), which is explained in v 8 as involving faith, love and hope. When Jesus returns, he will seek faith, love and hope—will he find it?

8. What is the reason for Christian hope in the face of God's wrath (see also 1 v 10)? Christians have not been appointed for wrath but for salvation (v 9) because Jesus died for us so that we might live with him (v 10). This may be a good point at which to check how much the people in your group really understand about how Jesus, through his death on the cross, rescues us from the coming wrath.

EXPLORE MORE
Read the following passages, and consider how the Old Testament prophets had encouraged the people to prepare for the day of the Lord?
Isaiah 2 v 22: Do not trust in man.
Joel 2 v 12-14: Return to the Lord with

mourning for sin and seek his blessing. **Zephaniah 1 v 7** Be silent and consider a sacrifice the Lord has made (ie: Jesus!).

9. How do these verses inspire you to keep going as a Christian...

- **...when you become discouraged or weary in doing good?** We should remind ourselves that only the Christian life prepares us for the day of the Lord—a life of constant alertness and self-control, not one of relaxation and self-indulgence. The time for Christians to rest will be after Christ's return.

- **...when you find it hard to talk to people about the Christian message?** We need to remember that only those who believe in Jesus and become "children of light" will be rescued from the coming wrath. People around us, who seem happy enough as non-Christians, are utterly deluded and are heading for destruction.

- **...when money, comfort or leisure distracts you from the Christian faith?** When this happens, we have forgotten that none of these things can save us from the coming wrath, and if we live to pursue them we will not escape destruction when the day of the Lord comes.

10. Are you alarmed by the thought of the day of the Lord? Why, or why not? If we are Christians, living consistently with our faith (ie: alert and self-controlled, not complacent or indulgent), we need not be alarmed, because we can be both warned and prepared. Otherwise, we should be alarmed—the purpose of this warning is to make us understand that in Christ, we will be rescued from the coming wrath, and therefore motivate us to believe in him. However, some who live as Christians may still lack assurance, worrying that they are not a good enough Christian. Take the opportunity to emphasise that it is Christ and his work that rescues us from the coming wrath (1 v 10). The issue is not how good a Christian I am, but whether I trust in Christ to save me.

- **How will you "encourage one another and build each other up" this week?** Let's proactively encourage other Christians as we talk about these things. Talk about particular situations in which this could be appropriate.

7 1 Thessalonians 5 v 12-28
FAITH, LOVE AND HOPE

THE BIG IDEA
Be full of faith, love and hope in everyday life.

SUMMARY
Paul encourages the Thessalonians to have love for God's people (v 12-15), faith in God's provision (v 16-22) and hope in God's purpose (v 23-24). He then concludes (v 25-28) with personal comments.

Note: With so many different instructions in this passage, it would be easy to fail to see the wood for the trees. The "wood" could be summed up as: live the life of faith, love and hope in everyday life. The "trees" are the individual instructions. It might be sensible to major on three or four verses that seem particularly appropriate, but, if this is the case, try to cover the rest of the passage at speed to give the overall context.

OPTIONAL EXTRA
Imagine you were to read 1 Thessalonians with a younger Christian and study it together, perhaps once a week for a couple of months. How do you think they would benefit from this? How would it encourage them in their Christian life? Is this something you might be able to do? Perhaps pray for opportunities.

GUIDANCE FOR QUESTIONS
1. What does the average person in the street think goes on in church? Make a list together of the key things you would tell them. Likely answers may include: hymns; prayers; giving money; mass/eucharist; silence and contemplation etc. It is likely that the non-Christian view

of church will tend to focus on individuals doing religious stuff in a religious building. As will be seen, Paul's focus is on Christians together, demonstrating relationships and attitudes (not just activities) shaped by Christian faith, love and hope, in everyday life (not just in meetings or special buildings).

2. How should Christians love their leaders? Acknowledge (= respect) them (v 12) and hold them in the highest regard (v 13).

3. How should Christians love their fellow Christians? Live in peace (v 13); warn, encourage and help according to need (v 14); be patient (v 14); be kind, even when people wrong you (v 15).

4. APPLY: What are some of the reasons why Christians fail to respect their leaders? Reasons may include: failing to value the hard work that they do in teaching God's word and caring for the Christian family; lack of awareness of the sacrifices that are involved in doing this work; resentment at being challenged or admonished etc.

• **How will a life of Christian faith, love and hope enable us to follow Paul's instructions here?** A life shaped by Christian faith will help us to be grateful for God's provision of leaders and positive towards them. A life shaped by Christian love will help us to be alert to the sacrifices that our leaders make and the hardships that they may suffer, so that we look to support and encourage them (and their families); a life shaped by Christian hope will help us to remember that the most important thing in life is to be holy and blameless when Jesus Christ returns, and therefore to value the work of our leaders, and accept their admonitions.

5. APPLY: What are some of the reasons why Christians fail to treat fellow Christians as Paul instructs? Reasons why Christians fail to treat fellow-Christians as Paul instructs may include: allowing matters such as past grievances, jealousy or personality clashes to assume more importance than the unity and peace of God's people; failure to appreciate that building up the church is the most important work that we can do in this world, so that we are lazy or indifferent to helping one another; lack of assurance about our own salvation so that we feel unqualified to help fellow Christians etc.

• **How will a life of Christian faith, love and hope enable us to do this?** A life shaped by Christian faith will help us to be grateful for God's provision of Christian brothers and sisters to build us up. A life shaped by Christian love will want what is best for our brothers and sisters. A life shaped by Christian hope will help us to understand now what these people will be when Jesus returns, and motivate us to work towards that goal.

6. From v 16-18, how should our faith in God's provision show itself? We are always joyful (because God provides for our every need), always prayerful (because we depend on God for everything), and always thankful (because we trust that God provides what is best for us).

7. As well as daily needs, God provides for our greatest need—that we might know him. He does this through the sword of the Spirit, which is the word of God. How should we show our faith in God's provision for our spiritual needs through his word? Some people try to put the Spirit and the word as alternatives, so that "doing everything by The Book" is considered somehow "unspiritual". But the Spirit is the author of the Bible — they are his words! We do not put out the Spirit's fire by ignoring his ministry through the Scriptures. Indeed, v 21 says we should test all words of prophecy. By what? By the Scriptures of course. Other practical answers to this question will include:
• reading the Bible regularly.
• listening carefully to God's word preached and taught.
• memorising Scripture.
• using "the Spirit's sword" to preach to ourselves and others about Christ.

8. APPLY: How does the joyfulness, prayerfulness and thankfulness of Christians show their true faith in God? Joyfulness and thankfulness show that, regardless of circumstances, we are confident of the great things God has done for us in Jesus Christ, and the great hope that is stored up for us in eternity. Prayerfulness shows that we are confident of what God has done in making us a saved child of God, so that we can now approach our loving and all-powerful Father for provision of all our needs.

• **What helpful hints are given here to indicate what Christians should do when they meet together as church?** We should consider our attitude to our leaders and our attitudes to one another. We should rejoice in God's provision and put our trust in his ways of providing for us. This means that when we meet together we will spend time listening to God's word, praying, giving expression to our joy and thankfulness, accepting encouragement, challenge and admonition, offering help to one another according to need etc.

9. What will God do? He will sanctify us (make us holy), and he will keep us until Jesus returns.

10. Why can we be so confident that He will do it? He is faithful (so he will keep his promises) and he is able (so he can keep his promises).

11. APPLY: How do these two verses inspire you to keep going as a Christian? We can rest in God's promises, trusting him to keep us.

12. What impact do you imagine the reading of this letter would have had? These people wouldn't just be informed about how to keep going in the Christian faith—they would be fantastically motivated and helped to endure. And they would be equipped to recognise dangers and deal with them.

13. APPLY: What impact has studying this letter had on you? This is an opportunity for people to share the greatest encouragements and challenges from all the sessions. And in doing this, to put into practice right now Paul's instructions to encourage and help one another. Be personal and practical.

PRAY

By now the group should be quite familiar with the idea of reviewing what has been learned and identifying prayer points for praise and thanksgiving, confession and requests. As this is the final session, no suggestions have been given in the Leader's Guide. Instead, participants can review the whole of Paul's letter and select prayer items that have made the greatest impact.

Good Book Guides
The full range

1 Corinthians:
8 Studies
Andrew Wilson
ISBN: 9781784986254

2 Corinthians:
7 Studies
Gary Millar
ISBN: 9781784983895

Galatians: 7 Studies
Timothy Keller
ISBN: 9781908762566

Ephesians: 10 Studies
Thabiti Anyabwile
ISBN: 9781907377099

Ephesians: 8 Studies
Richard Coekin
ISBN: 9781910307694

Philippians: 7 Studies
Steven J. Lawson
ISBN: 9781784981181

Colossians: 6 Studies
Mark Meynell
ISBN: 9781906334246

1 Thessalonians:
7 Studies
Mark Wallace
ISBN: 9781904889533

1&2 Timothy: 7 Studies
Phillip Jensen
ISBN: 9781784980191

Titus: 5 Studies
Tim Chester
ISBN: 9781909919631

Hebrews: 8 Studies
Justin Buzzard
ISBN: 9781906334420

Hebrews: 8 Studies
Michael J. Kruger
ISBN: 9781784986049

James: 6 Studies
Sam Allberry
ISBN: 9781910307816

1 Peter: 6 Studies
Juan R. Sanchez
ISBN: 9781784980177

1 John: 7 Studies
Nathan Buttery
ISBN: 9781904889953

Revelation: 7 Studies
Tim Chester
ISBN: 9781910307021

TOPICAL

Man of God: 10 Studies
Anthony Bewes & Sam
Allberry
ISBN: 9781904889977

Biblical Womanhood:
10 Studies
Sarah Collins
ISBN: 9781907377532

The Apostles' Creed:
10 Studies
Tim Chester
ISBN: 9781905564415

**Promises Kept: Bible
Overview:** 9 Studies
Carl Laferton
ISBN: 9781908317933

The Reformation Solas
6 Studies
Jason Helopoulos
ISBN: 9781784981501

Contentment: 6 Studies
Anne Woodcock
ISBN: 9781905564668

Women of Faith:
8 Studies
Mary Davis
ISBN: 9781904889526

Meeting Jesus: 8 Studies
Jenna Kavonic
ISBN: 9781905564460

Heaven: 6 Studies
Andy Telfer
ISBN: 9781909919457

Making Work Work:
8 Studies
Marcus Nodder
ISBN: 9781908762894

The Holy Spirit: 8 Studies
Pete & Anne Woodcock
ISBN: 9781905564217

Experiencing God:
6 Studies
Tim Chester
ISBN: 9781906334437

Real Prayer: 7 Studies
Anne Woodcock
ISBN: 9781910307595

Mission: 7 Studies
Alan Purser
ISBN: 9781784983628

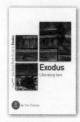

thegoodbook
COMPANY

BIBLICAL | RELEVANT | ACCESSIBLE

At The Good Book Company, we are dedicated to helping Christians and local churches grow. We believe that God's growth process always starts with hearing clearly what he has said to us through his timeless word—the Bible.

Ever since we opened our doors in 1991, we have been striving to produce Bible-based resources that bring glory to God. We have grown to become an international provider of user-friendly resources to the Christian community, with believers of all backgrounds and denominations using our books, Bible studies, devotionals, evangelistic resources, and DVD-based courses.

We want to equip ordinary Christians to live for Christ day by day, and churches to grow in their knowledge of God, their love for one another, and the effectiveness of their outreach.

Call us for a discussion of your needs or visit one of our local websites for more information on the resources and services we provide.

Your friends at The Good Book Company